Stop Smoking

Hypnotherapy For Healing: Effective Techniques To
Address Weight Management And Smoking Cessation

*(The Female Individual Who Purchased A Residence
Utilizing Her Earnings From Tobacco Products Infers How
One Can Cease The Habit Of Smoking)*

Stanislaw Gattringer

TABLE OF CONTENT

Is It Feasible To Resign Within A 30-Day Period?..... 1

Rationales For Making The Decision To Cease Smoking 14

Approaches To Facilitate Smoking Cessation 41

Exploring The Factors Behind Smoking: Behavioral Dependence................49

Defining Triggers 55

What Are The Appropriate Measures To Take In The Event Of A Slip Or Relapse? 63

May I Inquire As To The Date On Which You Initiated The Practice Of Smoking? 85

A Rational Intellect Refrains From Harming Its Possessor................97

Appropriate Approaches To Cease Smoking 125

The Hard Habit Awareness................135

What Is The Extent Of The Potential Harm It Can Cause?................159

Is It Feasible To Resign Within A 30-Day Period?

Although there is widespread awareness that smoking is the primary cause of preventable deaths nationwide, a significant number of smokers encounter challenges when attempting to cease this habit. To be honest, a stunning 50 million Americans are sustaining the tobacco industry through their persistent engagement in regular cigarette consumption. And that is merely an approximation. Regrettably, it must be noted that the aforementioned figures continue to increase at an indeterminate pace, with an alarming trend of smokers becoming progressively younger.

It is customary for smokers to include the cessation of smoking as a recurring item on their New Year's resolutions list each year. Numerous individuals hold aspirations of achieving smoke-free status, or transitioning into a state of being an ex-smoker within a span of 30 days. The question at hand pertains to the possibility of such an endeavor. Within the contents of this book, readers will be provided with pragmatic recommendations on how to accomplish this task. If you currently engage in smoking and desire to permanently relinquish this deleterious habit with minimal discomfort, this compendium is tailored specifically for you.

Experts behind the program

The development of the 30-day smoking cessation program is the result of a collaborative effort among a team of experts. One individual among them is a former smoker who has successfully conquered his habit through the utilization of various techniques and personal revelations throughout his journey. Conversely, there exists a medical practitioner whose parents perished due to lung cancer, which was directly caused by the habit of smoking tobacco. These advocates collaborated closely with individuals who continue to engage in smoking behavior. Significant modifications have been noted among the participants, a majority of whom demonstrated success in refraining from tobacco use as a result of employing the respective methodologies.

What are the principal attributes of the 30-day smoking cessation program?

Typically, in alternative cessation programs, individuals who smoke are mandated to adhere to predetermined sets of tasks and activities. Their rigidity hinders adaptability, leading to a high turnover rate driven by employee disillusionment. In this 30-day program, participants will gain a comprehensive understanding of a set of principles and exemplary behaviors. These valuable insights will serve as a guiding framework to determine their next actions. Beyond the discrete measures, it is of paramount importance to acknowledge the imperative nature of abstaining from smoking.

Additionally, the individuals who have chosen to stop smoking are equipped with real-life instances, encompassing both positive and negative outcomes. This text highlighted instances where individuals who successfully abstained from the habit experienced notable improvements in their overall wellbeing. However, it is important to consider the perspectives and circumstances of individuals who consciously opted to indulge in the act of smoking, as well as the detrimental consequences associated with this habit. The following accounts convey the experiences of both individuals who encountered substantial difficulties in quitting, as well as those who traversed the process smoothly. The individuals who smoke will be provided with a targeted set of abilities to enhance their determination to achieve their modest aspiration of relinquishing the detrimental habit.

Furthermore, this program does not endorse a singular methodology. It supports the notion of a paradigm shift while acknowledging that a greater range of supplementary approaches, strategies, and techniques can enhance the likelihood and efficacy of swift and thorough cessation. Thus, this encompasses more than merely fostering a positive perspective or employing pharmaceutical interventions. This program acknowledges the efficacy of both approaches when applied appropriately.

The process of strengthening ought to originate internally rather than being reversed. The cultivation of inner resilience shall empower those who possess the discernment and determination required to partake in this program, enabling them not only to permanently abstain from smoking but also to augment their self-value. This program will serve to facilitate the cultivation of self-confidence, a critical attribute required to confront and overcome all manner of challenges.

A considerable number of individuals perceive the notion of ceasing smoking within a thirty-day timeframe as utterly incredulous. Is it even possible?

It is possible. To be completely honest, the act of cessation is undeniably simple.

However, it is the ramifications of ceasing that pose the true adversary. Based on the accounts of individuals who have abstained, the key challenge they encounter revolves around adapting to a smoke-free existence with utmost ease. Smoking encompasses both addictive properties and habitual tendencies. Although addictions may be treated, habits require replacement or unlearning. To execute this effectively, one must possess a heightened degree of self-awareness.

What is the underlying mechanism driving the effectiveness of the 30-day program?

Apologies for dispelling any illusions, but it is important to note that there is no supernatural element at play in this procedure. Ceasing the act of smoking is not akin to merely extinguishing a lit candle; the process is far from being of such simplicity. However, there is an undisclosed strategy: cultivating self-assurance. Once a program participant succeeds in enhancing their confidence, they will discover the resilience required to persevere through the challenging journey of quitting. As long as individuals possess a sense of self-assurance, they will increasingly discover additional motivations to persevere in overcoming the formidable obstacle of ceasing a particular behavior.

Why do individuals persist in engaging in smoking behaviours, despite being aware of the detrimental impact it can have on their health, and worse, its potential fatality?

There exist individuals who experience respiratory ailments, such as asthma, cardiac disorders, and specific forms of malignancies. Nevertheless, they persist in their smoking habits. They possess unequivocal knowledge that smoking would not be beneficial to them and their condition, yet their rationality is being overridden by the grip of addiction.

In addition to the diminishing rationality, false notions regarding health are disseminated to endorse the habit of smoking. For instance, it is widely believed that smoking alleviates their stress. Alternatively, a considerable number among them hold the belief that its consumption aids in the enhancement of their digestive processes. Some individuals believe that smoking can enhance their creativity and stimulate the generation of novel ideas.

If they were only acquainted with the actual account, they would be inclined to abstain from igniting another tobacco stick.

Rationales For Making The Decision To Cease Smoking

Smoking can harm your health, as cigarettes contain nicotine, which is highly addictive. However, being preoccupied with other matters should not serve as a justification for one's inability to quit smoking. Multiple studies have consistently demonstrated that smoking poses a significant health risk. Consequently, there is no logical justification for individuals who are already dependent on this habit to not cease their smoking behavior.

It is imperative to renounce smoking. Individuals typically make multiple attempts before successfully quitting smoking, usually ranging from two to three tries. It demands unwavering dedication and substantial effort, but with absolute determination, one can permanently quit smoking.

Why quit smoking? There exist a minimum of five justifications as to why you should discontinue the habit of smoking. Therefore, the pressing and most crucial query to ponder is "how can I cease the habit of smoking?" Herein lie five strategies that may aid in the cessation of smoking: It is possible for anyone to successfully quit this harmful habit, therefore, do not hesitate to make an effort to bring an end to smoking as well. Cease your smoking habit immediately, and I assure you a life of enhanced health, greater stature, and utmost prosperity.

2

Incorporate herbal remedies to aid in smoking cessation.

H

erbs

cab help

This program aims to facilitate your smoking cessation effortlessly. It is no longer necessary to enroll in a course for the treatment of nicotine addiction, as these herbs offer a comprehensive alternative solution.

It is widely recognized that smoking has adverse effects on one's health. Certain individuals who possess the habit of smoking are in need of abstaining from this particular activity, although they encounter significant challenges in doing so. If enrolling in a smoking cessation program is prohibitively expensive, these herbal remedies provide a cost-effective alternative. This presents a favorable opportunity to initiate the process of smoking cessation.

Chapter One

Will Power

One can exert dominion over their thoughts and actions through the utilization of an innate form of fortitude referred to as willpower. Willpower may be defined as a comprehensive ability for self-determination, as one's will constitutes their capacity to consciously determine their chosen course of action. Willpower transcends mere skill, enabling individuals to overcome temptation and follow through with resolutions despite any inclinations to do otherwise. Examples of elementary exercises in self-control entail refraining from indulging in the ice cream stored in the freezer or exhibiting poise when confronted with anger.

Mental resilience is frequently regarded as a manifestation of strong determination. Self-discipline, particularly in the presence of a strong desire, is the ability to rationalize abstaining from smoking and convince oneself to continue as a non-smoker. Each individual possesses a certain degree of determination as they embark on their endeavor to quit, and every individual will have to draw upon a portion of that determination to resist cravings. Implementing a resolute determination initiative should be a pivotal element within your comprehensive plan to cease smoking. Moreover, by amalgamating potent willpower techniques with any of the scientifically substantiated cessation methods delineated in this literature, your chances of achieving success will be significantly magnified. One advantageous aspect of employing willpower techniques is their inherent cost-effectiveness and accessibility, as they can be readily accessed without incurring any financial burdens, such as when facing sudden cravings. Your cognitive faculties are all that is requisite.

What strategies can be employed to effectively manage and suppress one's cravings through the utilization of self-control?

When endeavoring to manage smoking cravings, the utilization of willpower techniques can prove highly efficacious. As an illustration, let us contemplate the subsequent scenario:

When a sudden desire emerges, a fraction of your brain prompts you,

"Indeed, you may indulge in a solitary cigarette without detriment." However, it is possible to counter this notion by incorporating alternative perspectives to quieten that alluring voice until the craving diminishes. Contemplate a hypothetical scenario, such as "Should I engage in smoking one cigarette today, I will invariably succumb to resuming the habit." I have made significant progress and reached a critical point where I cannot afford to make any errors, therefore, I strongly oppose the possibility of making such a mistake. The constructive concepts that counteract your cravings can enhance your motivation to persevere after achieving success in overcoming the habit of smoking.

Effective tactics through the application of determination

It is imperative to possess a repertoire of potent willpower strategies to effectively regulate your cravings during their duration, as the impulses for nicotine or smoking can prove arduous to manage and are quite pervasive upon initial cessation. One can continually acquire new skills to enhance their self-discipline, as not all individuals employ identical approaches. Presented below are several strategies conducive to cultivating and harnessing one's willpower, which may prove beneficial to you. Incorporating these techniques into your routine can prove invaluable in combating cravings and sustaining your motivation.

Harness your inherent cognitive abilities or integrate them with any of the empirically validated techniques or strategies outlined in this publication.

1. Exhibiting the determination to decline: Identify a suitable setting wherein you may peacefully sit undisturbed for a duration of 5 minutes. Please close your eyes and relax. Consider yourself as a film. In this film, you observe a customary circumstance in which you find yourself in the company of another individual - be it a romantic partner, acquaintance, or

colleague - with whom it is customary to engage in smoking activities. You are determined to adhere to your decision to cease smoking. However, you are nonetheless inclined to succumb and ignite.

Another individual suggests indulging in the act of smoking a cigarette. Would you care to step outside and indulge in a cigarette? You are capable of perceiving their requests.

Subsequently, mentally envision yourself responding to this individual with phrases such as "I appreciate the offer, but I do not partake in smoking" or "Thank you for your kind gesture, however, I am a non-smoker."

Repeat this exercise. Mentally reiterate the phrases "I kindly decline, as I do not partake in smoking" or "I respectfully decline, as I identify as a non-smoker." Please acknowledge the gratification derived from demonstrating steadfastness in your approach. Shift your focus to the present moment. Invoke the memory of this film whenever you perceive a risk to the efficacy of your smoking cessation plan.

2. Reflecting on Your Life's Journey: Seek out a serene environment where you can comfortably settle for five uninterrupted minutes. Close your eyes and allow yourself to relax. Envision, if you will, that your existence unfolds as a narrative bestowed with diverse potential conclusions. In this film, your character is depicted as someone who refrained from making any earnest attempts to cease smoking as their life

progressed. Consider a scenario in which you possess

Expeditiously advanced the timeline of this film by a span of 10 to 20 years. You come to a halt in the film at a particular juncture. This specific occurrence highlights the utmost adverse implications of smoking on an individual's life, encompassing aspects such as their well-being and financial circumstances, among others. What is your perception of this image?

How are you doing? In what troublesome situation do you find yourself? Could you kindly provide information about the other individuals depicted in the photograph? What are the facial expressions, if any, displayed by the other individuals when they cast a fleeting gaze upon you? Take some time to carefully contemplate this image; it ought to provide significance to you. Please collect all the necessary information gradually and with careful consideration. Please ensure that the image is of high clarity. Open your eyes now. Envision this scenario whenever you perceive that your efforts to cease smoking may be at risk.

3. I Elect to Abstain from Smoking: Enhancing Self-Confidence" It is common to experience a sense of self-deprivation or the absence of a coping mechanism when one initially endeavors to cease smoking, particularly when

witnessing others engaged in smoking and developing a craving.

Consider, for example, the scenario where you find yourself at a social event or when your workday has been filled with considerable stress. One can notice an individual indulging in smoking outdoors while absorbing the occasion or alleviating their stress. I covet their possessions; you are inclined to believe.

But here lies the key: Why not consider it as your choice to abstain from smoking, rather than perceiving it as denying yourself a reward by saying, 'I cannot smoke.' In essence, you still possess the ability to ignite a cigarette. Nonetheless, at present, you choose not to engage in the act of smoking. Please attempt the subsequent exercise:

Envision a typical scenario wherein you may find yourself in the presence of fellow individuals partaking in smoking whilst gently shutting your eyelids. Perhaps following a demanding day.

Are you referring to a professional setting or a social gathering? Your attention is drawn to an individual engaging in the act of smoking. You experience an abrupt and compelling desire. Please mentally affirm the following statement: "Although I may have the inclination to indulge in a cigarette, I conscientiously opt against partaking in smoking." I exercise my autonomy to make affirmative choices since I have renounced this habit. Individuals who smoke exhibit a compulsive behavior and lack alternative choices. Therefore, I am responsible in the absence of the smoker. After internalizing this, you will no longer experience the sensation of being deprived. This task can be performed at your convenience in order to actively promote the concept of abstaining from smoking.

4. Resist the Urge to Smoke: Utilizing "contradictory thoughts" can prove to be an immensely efficacious method for bolstering one's determination when faced with a craving for cigarettes. Please refer to the following compilation of willpower strategies in order to determine which ones best facilitate your ability to resist cravings:

Carefully consider each idea individually.

Following each instruction, kindly close your eyes and engage in a mental exercise wherein you visualize a specific environment wherein it is customary for you to partake in smoking, such as immediately after a meal.

Continue to hold that same thought.

There is a strong likelihood that I will resume smoking if I were to consume even a single cigarette. That does not align with my desired outcome.

I am reluctant to return at this point as I have made substantial progress.

I am experiencing a strong desire for a cigarette; however, I am committed to maintaining a smoke-free lifestyle due to the following reasons...

There is an appetite present, but it shall subside with time. Desires are temporary and do not endure indefinitely.

My mind is compelling me to engage in smoking due to this craving. I have no need nor inclination to engage in smoking.

"Even one cigarette hurts. In contrast, I will engage in the utilization of nicotine replacement therapy.

"I am powerful. I'm up for this".

I do not engage in smoking, therefore."

I abstain from the consumption of tobacco.

I desire to preserve my well-being.

I would encourage you to contemplate your self-control when confronted with a longing for nicotine.

Efforts can be made to address the issue of smoking. How?

Fortunately, there exists a plethora of herbal cessation remedies that can alleviate the discomfort experienced by individuals striving to quit smoking. In contemporary times, irrespective of the nature of one's health concern, herbal remedies are favored over their artificially synthesized counterparts. Such efficacy of herbal products can be attributed to their composition comprising solely of natural ingredients, ensuring a lack of adverse effects.

Some of the herbal remedies available for smoking cessation include herbal patches that function similarly to nicotine patches, inhalers, gums, herbal chews, and lozenges. Another advantageous aspect of these smoking cessation products lies in their compatibility with other herbal products aimed at achieving the same objective.

Once you have made the determination to cease smoking, the herbal treatments for smoking cessation should serve as your valuable accomplices on the path to recovery. Commencing the process of quitting smoking at an earlier stage will expedite the clearance of the accumulated effects of tobacco consumption within your lungs. You will experience immense satisfaction as the choice to remain nicotine-free will enhance the quality and duration of your life, fostering optimal health and well-being.

Discover effective and naturally-derived home remedies and techniques for quitting smoking

Ceasing the habit of smoking is a formidable challenge, particularly for individuals who have made previous attempts or are currently in the process of doing so. It is crucial for individuals to be aware of the intricate nature involved in extracting cigarettes from one's existence. There exists a multitude of approaches for ceasing the behavior. While certain individuals opt for self-regulation through cognitive means, others avail themselves of specialized healthcare facilities, nicotine patches, chewing gum, and alternative approaches. If your objective is smoking cessation and you are endeavoring to achieve it, this domestic remedy may serve as a beneficial supplement to facilitate this arduous endeavor. Kindly acquire the listed ingredients provided below and prepare yourself to consume this meal on a daily basis until your desired achievement is attained.

Combine the red onions and honey in the blender. Under the premise of subjecting all components to liquefaction, proceed to transfer the resulting mixture into a container, subsequently placing it in a refrigeration unit for a duration of two to three days. Subsequently, I recommend consuming solely a small dosage of this concoction for a maximum duration of nine days. Engaging in smoking can have comprehensive detrimental effects on the body, posing a heightened risk to overall health. This is particularly noteworthy considering that smoking contributes to 50% of lung cancer-related fatalities.

If you are seeking to cease smoking without recourse to any deleterious substances, EffectsOfDrugs.Info proposes alternative remedies such as medicinal plants which aid in overcoming the smoking habit. The stevia, valerian, verbena, linden, balm, and passiflora are the plants that hold utmost significance in attaining these objectives. These botanical specimens are utilized for their inherent sedative qualities, facilitating the attainment of restful sleep and ameliorating consequent withdrawal symptoms. It is equally imperative to commence contemplation of incorporating apples into your dietary habits, even if they are currently absent from your regimen and you aspire to cease smoking. Consuming a minimum of three apples on a daily basis aids in diminishing the craving to smoke and gradually renders it distasteful. You may consider experimenting with the use of carrots as an alternative, as they can effectively act as a substitute when the urge to smoke becomes overpowering. Carrots have the added benefit of facilitating detoxification. In the event that carrots are not to your liking, licorice can serve as a suitable replacement.

Ultimately, Noni juice serves as an effective remedy to counter nicotine addiction. Therefore, if the notion of resigning is contemplated, we hereby present a selection of organic approaches that have been researched and endorsed.

Approaches To Facilitate Smoking Cessation

Various methodologies exist for achieving long-term cessation of smoking. Certain individuals abruptly resign from their positions. They have made the decision to resign, and it proves to be advantageous for them. Some individuals gradually reduce their cigarette consumption over a prescribed duration until they ultimately cease smoking entirely. Some individuals opt for the utilization of nicotine patches in order to gradually lessen their nicotine intake. For individuals who smoke, alternative therapy proves to be the most effective approach. This encompasses the utilization of techniques such as hypnosis, acupuncture, or counseling.

It is possible that you may need to experiment with various approaches until you discover the most effective method to overcome your nicotine addiction and cease smoking.

Pharmaceutical Intervention for Smoking Cessation

The utilization of medication for smoking cessation can effectively alleviate withdrawal symptoms and effectively curb cravings. The efficacy of most medication is enhanced when it is incorporated into a comprehensive treatment regimen, complemented by regular medical supervision.

Nicotine Replacement Therapy

This necessitates utilizing nicotine substitutes in lieu of engaging in smoking. Illustrations of such alternatives include nicotine gum or nicotine patches. This essentially involves administering controlled, periodic doses of nicotine to mitigate the symptoms of withdrawal, while avoiding exposure to the harmful substances found in cigarettes. The objective of this therapeutic approach is to eradicate the psychological dependency on smoking among individuals who smoke, alongside fostering the acquisition of alternative coping mechanisms.

Non-nicotine Medication

There exist pharmaceutical treatments that can aid individuals in quitting smoking by mitigating both the intense desire to smoke and the unpleasant symptoms associated with withdrawal. Bupropion and varenicline serve as instances in illustrating this concept. It is crucial to emphasize that these medications should exclusively be utilized for a limited duration.

Alternative Method for Smoking Cessation

In the event that you are not convinced of the potential efficacy of the treatment mentioned earlier, you may consider exploring alternative therapies as a means to effectively address your nicotine addiction and successfully quit smoking.

Hypnosis

Hypnosis has proven to be efficacious in facilitating smoking cessation among a substantial number of individuals. The objective of hypnosis is to induce a state of deep relaxation, in which individuals are more receptive to suggestions aimed at aiding them in smoking cessation.

Additionally, it seeks to solidify your aversion towards smoking.

Acupuncture

Acupuncture is a time-honored therapeutic modality that promotes relaxation through the stimulation of endorphin release within the body. Acupuncture has been shown to effectively alleviate withdrawal symptoms and aid individuals in their efforts to quit smoking.

Motivational Therapies

This entails engaging in the activity of reading self-help literature or accessing online platforms specifically designed to provide motivation for quitting smoking. A compelling rationale presented by these resources aims to persuade individuals to quit smoking is of an economic nature. Written materials or online platforms demonstrate the substantial amount of money that can be saved by eliminating the smoking habit, which frequently serves as a convincing incentive for smokers to cease this detrimental behavior.

Do Not Turn to Smokeless Tobacco or Chewing Tobacco as a Method to Quit Smoking

Smokeless tobacco, also referred to as spit tobacco, does not serve as a viable healthier substitute for smoking cigarettes. This is due to the presence of identical harmful compounds found in cigarettes, which enable it to administer nicotine levels that are three to four times higher than those delivered by cigarettes.

Exploring The Factors Behind Smoking: Behavioral Dependence

Please bear in mind that the physiological dependency on nicotine constitutes merely one component of your dual dependency. The subsequent element pertains to your conduct. You demonstrate a strong dependency on smoking, comparable to the consistent indulgence in ice cream where an individual continues to consume it regularly for the indefinite span of time. Your smoking habit is so deeply rooted that even in the absence of physical nicotine withdrawal symptoms, you still experience a desire for a cigarette. Let's find out why.

Gaining Insight into the Formation of Behavioral Patterns

It is likely that you are familiar with the commonly held belief that it requires a period of 21 days to establish a habit. This statement is largely accurate, allowing for some flexibility based on the level of complexity involved in establishing the desired habit. Nevertheless, this 21-day guideline is equally applicable to both positive and negative behavioral patterns. When embarking on the journey of smoking cessation, it is imperative to acknowledge the multifaceted nature of the task at hand. One must not only confront the formidable challenge of unlearning deeply ingrained habits acquired over a span of years, or even decades, but also endeavor to cultivate alternative behaviors to fill the void left by relinquishing those habits. Outlined below are several illustrative instances.

EXAMPLE ONE: It is imperative to engage in smoking following each and every meal. Once you have finished your meal, you promptly assume a seated position and proceed to ignite a cigarette. This phenomenon occurs as a result of the consumption and subsequent digestion of food, causing a reduction in the nicotine present within your bloodstream, thus leading to your acquired knowledge. Your adoption of this behavior stems from a physiological reliance on cigarettes, and even in the absence of the physical craving, the behavior endures.

Alternate phrasing: "In the presence of alcohol, your smoking consumption appears to escalate." Numerous theories exist concerning the correlation between increased smoking and alcohol consumption. One of the theories postulates that alcohol increases the potency of the reward signal elicited by nicotine, although concrete evidence is currently lacking. Irrespective of the cause, a vast majority of individuals who partake in both smoking and consumption of alcohol tend to experience an increased intake of cigarettes during the act of drinking. Despite the absence of nicotine from the body, the conduct continues to persist. As you are indulging in alcoholic beverages, your cognitive faculties perceive a perceived correlation between the act of drinking and the necessity to partake in smoking a cigarette. Furthermore, when considering the influence of alcohol on willpower, one can easily recognize it as a contributing factor to the propensity for smoking. With the exception of modifying the conduct, however.

Behavioral Patterns and "Cues"

The stimuli that trigger smoking behavior are referred to as "cues". You have conditioned your brain to anticipate the consumption of a cigarette at specific intervals or following particular activities. Once the brain becomes cognizant of the impending moment or the execution of the task at hand, it dispatches a signal to notify you of the necessity to indulge in the act of smoking a cigarette. Why? The reason for this is simply due to the longstanding tradition.

Manipulating the Cognitive Process to Elicit Varied Neural Responses

To effectively diminish cigarette cravings triggered by a cue, it is imperative to substitute the existing association. It is imperative that you train your brain to anticipate an entirely different response upon receiving a signal, such as following a meal, during a telephone conversation, while operating a vehicle, or when consuming alcoholic beverages. We will delve into the precise process of achieving this in a subsequent chapter.

Defining Triggers

As we proceed with our recovery plan, it will be essential to identify and steer clear of triggers. Triggers encompass any stimuli capable of eliciting a strong desire or impulse to engage in smoking. Various individuals, locations, objects, or even contemplations possess the capacity to steer one towards a desire to ignite once more. We should exercise prudence in devising our itinerary and in determining the suitable environment. An illustration of a catalyst is when an individual with alcohol addiction passes by a bar they used to visit frequently, resulting in a stimulus that instigates a strong desire within them, ultimately compelling them to enter the bar with the intention of consuming "only one drink."

When attempting to cease the consumption of a substance, it is crucial to bear in mind that relapsing even once can result in a subsequent relapse, and this pattern may continue to escalate. Managing triggers promptly as they arise, effectively curbing the associated cravings and preventing the indulgence in further smoking, constitutes an important undertaking.

To effectively overcome urges and cravings, a proactive approach towards mental preparedness is indispensable. It is a well-established fact that individuals often encounter challenges when their minds deceive them and present a formidable obstacle to quitting smoking. The main objective is to facilitate the assimilation of careful consideration.

Preventing oneself from being taken off guard by unexpected cognitive impairment is advisable.

The array of illusions my mind endeavored to deceive me with primarily revolved around notions such as "What purpose is there, I derive pleasure from smoking," or perhaps the perilous notion of "Just one." The psychological stress caused by feelings of anger and anxiety will also have an impact. In instances when an extended period of time has transpired without the consumption of a cigarette, an individual may experience irritation or agitated feelings upon encountering certain individuals, scenarios, or even in the absence of any discernible cause. You respond in an unfavorable manner. That encapsulates the fervent anger and overwhelming anxiety to which I am referring; indeed, its impact can be severe. Prepare for these times.

You must adopt new behavioral patterns in order to effectively overcome various triggers.

Once more, as reiterated on numerous occasions, engaging in actions will contribute to the development of our thoughts. How do you typically respond when experiencing anger and feeling the urge to physically strike or vocalize distress? You act. The alternative behaviors to substitute angry, anxious, and depressive responses will vary for you compared to my own experience. If circumstances permit, I would promptly depart through the exit and partake in an extended stroll, if necessary. In instances when I found myself unable to ambulate, I would purposefully pause my activities and engage in the act of transcribing my emotions, thereby diminishing their influence over me. I would also exhibit mindfulness towards my cognitive processes and respiratory patterns. Later in the book, specifically in the chapter devoted to Exercise, readers will have the opportunity to explore various methodologies for engaging in mindful breathing.

Understanding triggers enables one to proactively devise strategies to effectively address and overcome them. I would recommend adopting a more deliberate and mindful approach, allowing yourself to fully appreciate and acknowledge each moment of the day that prompts you to indulge in smoking. Please transcribe the information by documenting each trigger that you are able to identify. Additionally, it is imperative to take into consideration elements that may not immediately register as triggers. Advertisements on television may act as a stimulus or even be integrated within the program, featuring a character engaging in smoking. List all triggers.

A crucial step, surpassing the mere enumeration of triggers, lies in elaborating upon each one with an accompanying strategy on redirecting one's focus to alternative pursuits, thereby effectively resisting temptation. Please provide annotations for any potential strategies that have been proven effective for your specific circumstances. On certain occasions, the optimal course of action entails expeditiously distancing oneself from the vicinity of the stimulus.

Other Ideas

Jotting down your thoughts would prove to be highly beneficial as you traverse through the course of your day. One might engage in activities such as showering, engaging in physical exercise, or pursuing other incompatible activities with the act of smoking. Unanticipated thoughts may arise without prior indication. That thought can start a chain of thoughts that lead you straight to the store, and suddenly in the back alley, puffing on a cigarette like it's the straw of a thick milkshake, not knowing how you got there. Be aware!

Summary

I continually emphasize the significance of labeling and devising strategies for every aspect within your surroundings and your thoughts.

that will assist you in avoiding contact with the smoke. You derived immense pleasure from it, yet it caused you greater pain than anyone else possibly could. Play it smart. Have a plan.

Few things have the potential to accelerate a relapse among individuals struggling with addiction as swiftly as the evocative influences of familiar individuals, locations, items, or thoughts. In times of adversity, make contact with individuals around you. Develop alternative strategies to address the adverse stimuli, and persistently overcoming one trigger without yielding to its influence will facilitate a subsequent resistance to succumbing to such triggers in the future.

What Are The Appropriate Measures To Take In The Event Of A Slip Or Relapse?

Under certain circumstances, it is possible to succumb to one's indulgences. What would be the case if you were to resume smoking? Let this serve as a source of encouragement to make another attempt, a misstep that can be readily rectified. Experiencing a minor setback or a complete regression does not imply that you are incapable of returning to a state of progress. Considering your previous success, it is evident that future iterations will yield even better outcomes, given your heightened understanding of the circumstances. You still retain authority.

Contemplate the stimuli that precipitated the occurrence of the slip or relapse. Examine how you succumbed to these influences and adapt your smoking cessation strategy to eliminate these triggers entirely. Refrain from engaging in justifications that could rationalize your lapse or relapse, such as the following:

I must come to terms with my inability to overcome this addiction, as it will likely persist throughout my existence.

Committing an error does not imply that you are an unsuccessful individual. You can continually avail yourself of your Stop Smoking Program. According to the observations of experts, the initial attempt serves as an opportunity for practice, while the subsequent attempt can also be regarded as a practice session. However, it is typically after the third or fourth endeavor that one eventually achieves the desired outcome. Just don't give up.

"It's my only vice. I am able to reconcile the situation through my adherence to healthy practices."

Please make an effort to recall the multitude of diseases to which you are vulnerable if you engage in smoking. Engaging in physical activity and consuming nutritious foods fail to mitigate the hazards linked to smoking.

Please seek guidance from a qualified medical professional and engage in conversations with your support network. Engage their assistance in identifying the cause of your trigger and developing strategies to effectively manage and respond to it in case of future occurrences. Now that you have gained a deeper understanding, you can consciously opt for the more optimistic path by choosing to abstain from smoking today and in the foreseeable future.

Conclusion

Ceasing smoking can be a challenging endeavor, yet with accurate knowledge and personal drive, it is entirely achievable. Presently, you have the opportunity to join the increasing population of individuals who have effectively abandoned their smoking addiction.

To conclude, presented below are several infallible recommendations that can guide you on your path to cessation of smoking:

Enumerate the factors underlying your decision to resign

Record the reasons for your desire to resign and ensure that you consistently carry them.

- Develop the belief that ceasing one's current endeavors invariably results in favorable outcomes.

Set a quit date

Make advance preparations several weeks prior to your planned cessation date. Inform all individuals of your intention to resign and express your desire for their encouragement and support.

Gradually decrease your consumption until your designated cessation date.

Please acquaint yourself with the obstacles that you will encounter

- The cessation process may be accompanied by uncomfortable withdrawal symptoms, smoking cues, and intense cravings. Possessing the knowledge on how to effectively handle them will bestow upon you a competitive edge.

In order to manage withdrawal symptoms and mitigate cravings:" "During the process of dealing with withdrawal symptoms and curbing cravings:" "To address withdrawal symptoms and counteract cravings:" "To effectively combat withdrawal symptoms and alleviate cravings:" "To handle withdrawal symptoms and reduce cravings:

Direct your focus elsewhere and engage in productive activities.

Use oral substitutes

Refrain from placing yourself in circumstances that could potentially elicit your desire to smoke.

Be active

Do relaxing activities

Use NRTs if necessary

In the event of a slip or relapse, refrain from succumbing to despair. It is certainly possible for you to perform the task once more. Engaging in the activity once imparts ample knowledge to be utilized for rectifying errors and resuming participation in the endeavor.

Ceasing the act of smoking holds great significance, as it can be likened to severing ties with a detrimental and harmful association. The act of smoking deprives individuals of their youthfulness, financial resources, interpersonal connections, and overall well-being, offering nothing more than fleeting moments of transient pleasure. It is imperative that you assume responsibility and assume command. Dispose of the cigarette butt and embrace an improved, more contented, and physically thriving existence, resulting in an elongated lifespan.

Chapter 4: The Procedural Sequence of Resignation

Resigning can be arduous, yet the process can become more manageable with a well-structured strategy in place. If one believes they have reached a point of readiness to discontinue, they might discover the subsequent suggestions to be of utility.

Fully dedicate yourself to your resolution to cease.

Upon making the decision to resign, it is imperative to adhere to it steadfastly. It is necessary to establish a particular timeframe. It is crucial to establish a precise date in order to progress towards your objective expeditiously. The absence of a defined timeframe will likely result in you becoming prone to procrastination and ultimately losing sight of your objective.

When selecting a cessation date, ensure that you allocate a sufficient amount of time for adequate preparation. It is imperative that you approach this transformative decision with a composed and receptive state of mind and heart. It is imperative to bear in mind that success in smoking cessation requires not only the possession of appropriate skills, but also the cultivation of unwavering confidence.

Furthermore, it is advised to avoid excessive delay in this matter. If the date you plan to quit is sufficiently distant, there is a risk of succumbing to procrastination or experiencing a change of heart. Furthermore, your motivation will diminish as a result. It is advisable to ensure that the proposed date of resignation does not exceed a period of two weeks.

It would be advisable to contemplate resigning on the initial day of the week, specifically a Monday. By adopting this approach, you can potentially enhance your confidence and motivation to effectively cease the desired behavior. The majority of individuals believe that commencing an activity on the initial day of the week imbues them with a renewed sense of possibility. Additionally, you may utilize this day as your designated option for resetting the date on which you aim to quit, initiating communication with your support group, or establishing fresh objectives.

Nevertheless, if you continue to encounter difficulty in permanently ceasing this habit, you may engage in the exercise of abstaining for a brief period until you feel fully prepared. There exists a wide array of programs that you can consider experimenting with.

Create a quit plan.

Tailor your cessation strategy to align with your individual requirements. By adopting this approach, you will be able to effectively maintain your confidence, motivation, and concentration towards achieving successful cessation. If you lack knowledge on the process of creating one, you may consult the plethora of accessible cessation plans available online and utilize them as points of reference or guidelines. It is advisable to devise a cessation strategy prior to embarking on the quitting process.

However, it is acceptable if you have already commenced and have only recently devised your cessation strategy. This quit plan can still be utilized to ensure you remain on the correct course. You are welcome to review your quit plan on any day you prefer, although it is highly advisable to do so on Mondays. As today marks the inaugural workday of the week, it presents an opportune occasion for reaffirming your commitment to your objective.

Reflect upon the justifications behind your decision to resign.

Each individual harbors unique motivations for desiring a tobacco-free lifestyle. May I inquire about the rationale behind your decision to resign? It is of great significance to maintain a genuine sense of self. Ascertain your true intentions and desired outcomes pertaining to this objective.

Additionally, you may consider reflecting upon the aspects of smoking that you find displeasing and the opportunities that elude you with each instance of smoking. Discover the impact of tobacco consumption on various aspects of your life, encompassing your physical well-being, familial relationships, social interactions, professional pursuits, financial stability, academic achievements, and numerous other spheres of influence. Moreover, consider the potential improvements your life may experience upon cessation of smoking.

In addition, there is a wealth of literature available that delves into the narratives of individuals who have effectively kicked the habit of smoking. Familiarize yourself with their challenges, values, and guidance. Their determination and positive attitude may serve as a source of inspiration for you. Their tales of triumph might serve as an impetus for you to persevere in your endeavor to achieve a smoke-free lifestyle.

Acquire the knowledge to effectively manage one's yearnings and stimuli.

Smokers frequently encounter a range of stimuli, encompassing individuals, actions, and settings, which elicit a desire or compulsion to engage in smoking.

Similarly, they frequently experience cravings, characterized by brief yet intense urges to indulge in smoking. The duration of these cravings typically spans only a few minutes. It is crucial to engage in advanced planning in order to adequately ready oneself for instances of cravings. Ensure that you possess the capacity to divert your attention towards alternative activities, thereby preventing the inclination to engage in smoking.

Acquire the knowledge and techniques necessary to manage the symptoms of nicotine withdrawal.

Upon cessation of tobacco use, your body initiates a response to adapt to this transformation. It is possible that you will encounter discomfort and experience a desire for nicotine. The adverse symptoms that you are experiencing are referred to as withdrawal symptoms.

Smokers often undergo withdrawal symptoms upon cessation. However, it is worth noting that the symptoms experienced by individuals may differ based on the method they have adopted to cease their consumption. Certain individuals opt to cease abruptly while others prefer to engage in a gradual cessation process with the assistance of counseling, medications, and other resources.

The human body gradually acclimates to the absence of nicotine throughout the withdrawal procedure. During the period of withdrawal, individuals may encounter challenges such as insomnia, depressive symptoms, irritability, heightened anxiety, restlessness, and diminished concentration abilities.

Consequently, you might experience an inclination to engage in smoking as a means to alleviate these sensations. Nevertheless, it is crucial to consider that smoking will exacerbate those conditions. Rest assured that these symptoms will eventually dissipate.

Nicotine replacement therapy is widely regarded as a mainstream approach for addressing nicotine withdrawal symptoms. It is offered in various manifestations, including patches, gums, nasal sprays, lozenges, and inhalers. They have the potential to greatly enhance your chances of permanently ceasing the habit. Most of these items are readily available at your nearby pharmacy without necessitating a doctor's prescription.

Over the course of time, scholars have observed that nicotine replacement therapy has proven to be effective and secure. Nevertheless, it is advised against for pregnant women, adolescents, and individuals with specific medical ailments. It is highly recommended that you seek the advice of a medical professional prior to attempting this approach.

Furthermore, ensure that you adhere strictly to the instructions provided on the packaging of your nicotine replacement device.

Acquire knowledge regarding the available alternatives for cessation of smoking.

Certain individuals possess the capability to cease a habit or addiction abruptly without any gradual reduction or assistance. Nevertheless, numerous individuals are not as fortunate. These individuals eventually undergo a relapse and revert to their former detrimental patterns.

Conduct a thorough investigation regarding the options at your disposal. As an illustration, one could explore initiatives like SmokefreeTXT. Additionally, utilizing applications such as quitSTART app and QuitGuide app is also a viable option. Additionally, individuals have the option of contacting helplines dedicated to smoking cessation, such as 1-877-44U-QUIT and 1-800-QUIT-NOW.

Notify your nearest and dearest individuals regarding your intention to cease tobacco consumption.

Ceasing tobacco consumption becomes significantly more convenient when one receives encouragement and assistance from one's relatives and intimate companions. Therefore, it is advisable that you communicate your intentions to quit and commit to maintaining a smoke-free lifestyle to them. You may also request their assistance, should you require any form of support from them.

For instance, they have the capacity to exert a positive influence on your lifestyle choices, encouraging the adoption of healthier habits while simultaneously serving as a deterrent from potential triggers. They can also provide periodic updates to ensure that they stay informed about your progress.

Giving up smoking is not inherently antithetical to maintaining an active social life. Close companions will comprehend your choice and refrain from extending invitations to venues and gatherings frequented by individuals who engage in smoking. Alternatively, they will extend invitations to engage in wholesome pursuits, such as patronizing eateries that prohibit smoking and attending a film screening.

If you are in the company of individuals who smoke and happen to be your acquaintances or family members, it would be appropriate to kindly request their abstinence from smoking in your presence. By adhering to this approach, you can effectively avoid succumbing to the temptation of smoking alongside them. Additionally, it would be imperative to instruct them not to offer you any cigarettes under any circumstances, regardless of your actions or requests. They ought to possess greater awareness to discourage you from succumbing to the temptation of smoking.

Moreover, you may seek the support and patience of your family and friends during the course of your cessation journey. Inform them that during the period of withdrawal symptoms, it is possible that your mood may not be optimal. We kindly request their assistance in resolving this situation, through their empathy, forbearance, and backing.

May I Inquire As To The Date On Which You Initiated The Practice Of Smoking?

Could you please recall the precise circumstances in which you initiated your smoking habit? I do. The year was 1955 during the summer season. At the time, I had reached the age of ten while my elder twin brothers, Wally and Al, had already turned eleven.

During the initial period of that summer, our family transitioned from Chicago to a recently constructed dwelling situated within a burgeoning suburban area that emerged in close proximity to Chicago's jurisdiction - specifically, Worth, Illinois.

Our new residence was situated at a distance of approximately fourteen miles from the bustling city of Chicago. It seemed as if we resided in an alternate reality. It was ideal for adolescent males. There were verdant lawns and recreational areas where one could engage in ball games.

We rode our bikes, swam, and fished in the nearby quarry. We harvested untamed strawberries and blackberries from the adjacent woodland preserves, constructed fire pits, and toasted franks and potatoes, immersing ourselves in the roles of cowboys or soldiers engaged in covert operations.

Throughout the entirety of the day, spanning from the first light of dawn until the descent of dusk, an incessant chorus of hammers, saws, and bulldozers reverberated ceaselessly within the vicinity, as diligent construction crews fervently erected multiple abodes encircling our own.

My siblings and I visited all of the newly developed sites and engaged in conversations with the skilled carpenters. They provided us with small pieces of timber, which we transported home using a wagon in order to construct a modest clubhouse within the confines of our backyard. Following some initial amateur efforts, Dad and Grandpa graciously assisted in transforming our clubhouse into a structurally sound and resilient edifice. We conducted a paint application in order to harmonize it with the architectural style of the residence.

That clubhouse serves as the place where we initiated the habit of tobacco consumption. I have vivid recollection of that day, as though it transpired just yesterday. My brother, Al, hurriedly entered our residence and informed me of the imperative need to rendezvous with Wally and him in the communal clubhouse.

Upon opening the entrance to the clubhouse, I was presented with a package of cigarettes by my sibling, Wally. "Here, Ken," he said. "These are for you. Today, my mother made a purchase of a carton. We retrieved three packages, one for each individual in our party."

Wow. I was shocked.

Our parents both smoked. My grandfathers both smoked. Every one of my aunts and uncles was an avid smoker. All of my elder cousins were smokers. All of the males residing in our vicinity engaged in the act of smoking.

Cigarettes were consistently promoted through television advertisements. The news presenters, performers, and even professional sports players engaged in smoking. At that particular moment in time, John Wayne, who was my preferred protagonist in films, consistently engaged in smoking. The chief executive of the United States engaged in the act of smoking. Even our local clergyman indulged in tobacco consumption.

It appeared to be the case that all adults engaged in smoking, while none of the children within my acquaintance who were of the same age shared this habit. I unveiled my packet of cigarettes as my siblings proceeded to unveil theirs.

I extracted a cigarette from its package and proceeded to ignite it employing a wooden stick match. Once I successfully ignited it, I proceeded to engage in a few ineffective inhalations. I experienced a sense of unease and a heightened sense of self-awareness. I came to the realization that I had witnessed innumerable individuals partake in the act of smoking an extensive number of cigarettes, while paradoxically lacking the knowledge of how to engage in the aforementioned behavior myself.

I have observed that smoking is a skill that necessitates acquiring through practical experience. The twins graciously demonstrated to me the proper technique of inhalation. After a period of time, I attained proficiency in that particular skill. We consecutively lit and consumed multiple cigarettes. I did not smoke a significant portion of my cigarette. I merely partook in a small inhalation from each item. However, I was steadily improving and determined that my smoking abilities were on par with those of my siblings. Collectively, we experienced bouts of coughing and spluttering, accompanied by dizziness and a general sense of unease.

Upon entering the premises at a later time, it became immediately evident to my mother that we had engaged in the act of smoking.

In addition to her potential realization that three packs of her cigarettes had gone missing, I am certain that the three of us appeared culpable and emitted a strong odor of tobacco smoke. During the course of the interrogation, I swiftly made my way to the bathroom and regurgitated. My siblings admitted and disclosed to our mother the veracity of their action of misappropriating her cigarettes.

Regrettably, our mother did not make a request for the return of the cigarettes or matches, thus necessitating the discreet preservation of these items within our clubhouse. On the subsequent day, I returned unaccompanied to the clubhouse and indulged in a cigarette. On this occasion, I refrained from experiencing emesis. I experienced a sense of esteem in achieving proficiency in smoking without incurring any sickness, as I aspired to match my brothers' aptitude in this activity.

Similar to any intricate conduct, the art of cigarette smoking necessitates one's adeptness through a process of experimentation, diligent exertion, and continuous honing of skills.

It appeared that there was a compelling force that drew me back to the clubhouse on a daily basis, compelling me to indulge in the consumption of at least one additional cigarette.

After a short span of time, I acquired the skill of smoking proficiently. I possessed the knowledge of proper cigarette handling and the technique of igniting it. I was knowledgeable in the art of respiration, encompassing both inhalation and exhalation. I possessed the aptitude to successfully create smoke rings. I possessed the knowledge of skillfully removing the ash from the tip of the cigarette. I possessed the knowledge of concealing my cigarette consumption from individuals of legal age.

I held the belief that smoking contributed to my status as a person of stature: someone who exudes greater maturity, intelligence, and refinement. I sought endorsement and validation from my elder siblings. If they engaged in smoking, I would also partake in such behavior.

I persisted in the habit of smoking until I reached the age of twenty-five. I had never contemplated relinquishing it under any circumstance. But I did. I have acquired the knowledge and techniques for effectively ceasing the habit of smoking, and I am prepared to impart this wisdom to you.

Regrettably, my brother Alexander did not experience the same level of good fortune. He persisted in smoking and subsequently developed esophageal cancer, an exceptionally lethal variant of the disease. He experienced a prolonged impairment in his ability to ingest food orally and required sustenance to be delivered through a gastric tube. He gradually succumbed to his ailments and passed away in an agonizing manner at the age of fifty-four.

At the time of composing this correspondence, I am nearing the age of seventy and find myself in a commendable state of physical well-being. This state of being can be attributed to my choice to cease smoking more than four decades ago.

I have witnessed the maturation, marriage, and parenthood of my offspring. I have derived immense pleasure from participating in the festivities surrounding the commencement, marital unions, christenings, scholarly achievements, of a total of seven progeny and two descendants. Regrettably, my sibling's life was cut short before he could fully experience the advantages of embracing a smoke-free lifestyle.

Get comfortable. Relax your body. Inhale deeply a few times. Revisit the time when you initially began engaging in the practice of smoking. Consider your initial endeavors at smoking. Reflect upon the journey from acquiring the knowledge of smoking to becoming an established smoker. Consider any efforts you have made in an endeavor to cease smoking.

A Rational Intellect Refrains From Harming Its Possessor.

Indeed, it is verifiable that a significant number of individuals resort to seeking costly counseling services, purchasing nicotine patches, or pursuing other methods that entail substantial financial expenditures in order to facilitate their cessation of smoking.

However, in order for one to achieve complete consciousness, it is imperative to maintain sobriety consistently. This is due to the fact that sobriety is the sole means through which human beings can exercise sound judgment and engage in rational thinking concerning their thoughts and actions. Exercising restraint over one's conduct is imperative for leading a respectable life, necessitating a state of mental sobriety.

The initiation of smoking can be attributed to a violation of sobriety; it is imperative to rectify this violation in order to regain complete self-regulation.

If I were to inquire about your perspective on the wisdom of initiating a smoking habit, it is reasonable to assume that you would respond in the negative. Furthermore, an examination of the factors that influenced your decision to commence smoking would likely reveal that your mental faculties were not functioning optimally during that period. Maybe it was the influence from peers, or the depiction of smoking as fashionable or sophisticated. Perhaps your parents or guardians were frequent smokers.

Whenever we fail to exercise sound judgment, we make ourselves vulnerable to adverse circumstances. Therefore, it is imperative that we ensure our consciousness remains uninterrupted at all times, with utmost diligence, in order to uphold complete responsibility for our actions.

Individuals who maintain their sobriety never succumb to the habit of smoking, as their sound discernment and astute discernment prevent them from willingly embracing such a detrimental vice.

The imperative in maintaining the sanctity of your physical self lies in cultivating a cognitive faculty that consistently exhibits rationality with regards to your personal welfare.

Do you believe that the emphysema patient was cognizant of the consequences of his decision to engage in smoking, resulting in detriment to his respiratory function? Alternatively, it could be stated in a formal tone as follows: "Furthermore, it is worth noting that the woman afflicted by a severe case of malignant ulcers experienced considerable discomfort and interpreted her mouth sensations as self-inflicted harm." single. time. she lit one up?

No, however, they unmistakably exhibited a blatant lack of consideration for their physical beings - their bodies - the moment they took their first puff of a cigarette. However, it is inherent that the mind did not perceive it in such a manner.

The functioning of the human body, including your own, is mainly influenced by the subconscious mind, while the conscious mind plays a supportive role in collaborating with the subconscious mind in matters related to bodily processes. With that being mentioned, it is crucial to note an exceedingly significant fact that often goes unnoticed by smokers attempting to quit. This oversight ultimately leads to their failure, namely, their utilization of methods that bypass the cognitive decision-making process.

However, rational reasoning indicates that it was a cognitive choice that led to your initiation of smoking. How prudent is it to endeavor to address the issue using any approach that fails to direct your focus inward to your thoughts?

A viable and intellectual approach exists to address the habit of smoking, and as the controller of your cognitive faculties, you need not indulge in futile experimentation that essentially harms your physiological functioning.

Apart from the health implications such as cancer and emphysema, the presence of foreign substances in cigarettes hinders the production of essential hormones that contribute to maintaining a state of equilibrium and societal refinement. This is the primary obstacle in obtaining assistance from your physical and mental faculties to cease the activity. You have effectively displaced the viable agents and substituted them with detrimental ones.

Prior to delving into the ultimate solution, let us first explore a selection of frequently employed techniques for smoking cessation.

Millions of individuals employ the subsequent strategies on a daily basis to effectively abandon their smoking habit. This affirms the notion that there exists a multitude of approaches to cease smoking, yet a consensus among former smokers suggests a singular verity...

You consistently demonstrate a desire to resign.

The prevailing approaches to smoking cessation:

1. Discontinuing abruptly or ceasing abruptly

2. Prescription medication or pills

3. Nicotine replacement therapy (NRT)

4. Zyban tablets

5. Gradual reduction technique or phased discontinuation

6. Hypnosis

7. Acupuncture

8. Laser therapy

9. Chantix program

10. Psychotherapy, counseling, vaporization, and similar interventions.

We observe diverse approaches employed by individuals as they diligently strive to overcome their addiction to smoking cigarettes. And it is evident that individuals' willingness to explore such ideas signifies a lack of cognitive discipline and limited command over their thought processes.

However, it is crucial to dedicate the necessary effort towards acquiring mastery over one's cognitive faculties, considering that quantum physics has demonstrated the creative influence of thoughts. If you persist in maintaining the belief in the addiction of your body, you will encounter significant challenges in effectively surmounting it.

Now, let us briefly examine the psychological factors at play in this situation. You inadvertently became ensnared in a heedless pattern, persisting in it until you succumbed to a grave dependency. Although you may have observed individuals ambulating with oxygen tanks and nasal tubing to facilitate respiration. Furthermore, despite being undoubtedly aware of the ample evidence of individuals succumbing to smoking-related ailments and conditions, you persistently failed to initiate any endeavors to cease your smoking habit.

For a considerable duration of time, ranging from possibly one year to as much as twenty years, you procured cigarettes with the same regularity as one would acquire sustenance. In some cases, the desire for a cigarette was so intense that certain individuals couldn't even contain themselves until the designated 10:30 AM break, often leaving their place of employment to satisfy their craving.

There are diverse interpretations of mental fortitude among individuals. For certain individuals, simply possessing the ability to commute from one's residence to the workplace is indicative of one's mental well-being. However, this is not true, as to function effectively consciousness must be balanced.

Additionally, this serves as the crucial factor in surmounting the manifestations of withdrawal stemming from the body's reliance on nicotine, as well as the ensuing yearnings to substitute smoking with misguided behavioral patterns.

The human mind is an exceptionally intricate and potent entity, and individuals who lack awareness of its inherent fragility and potency are likely to encounter significant adversity in their lives.

The Challenges of Ceasing an Activity

Smoking continues to be the foremost avoidable cause of numerous fatalities throughout the United States. However, if one is a smoker, one is aware that overcoming this habit is more challenging in practice than in theory. One can attribute responsibility to nicotine, an immensely addictive component found in tobacco products, which can induce emotional dependence and physical withdrawal.

Nevertheless, with the arrival of the New Year, the current period presents an ideal opportunity to actively engage in adhering to your resolution of quitting smoking. There is no reason to feel discouraged if you continue to encounter difficulty in overcoming the habit of smoking, as you are not alone in this endeavor. Indeed, this resolution ranks among the top five commonly made New Year's resolutions annually, indicating that there is a sizeable population with the same predicament as yourself. Prior to addressing any other matters, it is imperative to confront your addiction along with the accompanying habits. Commence by formulating a pragmatic strategy that will assist you in successfully navigating through this situation.

particular challenge.

Advanced Planning

Multiple factors have compelled you to arrive at this decision. To achieve success, this motivation must be fortified with a resolute and unwavering determination. Consult your schedule and select the optimal month devoid of stress for you to resign.

Establish a Supportive Community

Challenges are to be expected during the initial weeks, as you will need to confront and manage symptoms of withdrawal. You have the option to seek the support and aid of your family, friends, and colleagues. These individuals can serve as the finest source of encouragement and resilience amidst this daunting period. In addition, you have the option to participate in a support group.

Eliminate the Temptations

It is necessary to identify the factors that elicit the behavior of smoking. Steer clear of circumstances that may prompt you to reach for a cigarette and reduce the amount of time dedicated to socializing with individuals who engage in smoking. Please ensure the removal of cigarettes, as well as any other smoking paraphernalia and apparatus, from your vicinity.

Be Active

Engaging in physical pursuits will effectively distract you and keep you occupied whenever you feel the urge to smoke a cigarette. When you have an abundance of spare time, consider visiting the gym or partaking in a leisurely walk in the park.

Consult with a Professional

Additionally, you may consider seeking guidance from a behavioral therapist who can provide support in your journey towards cessation.

Alternatively, you may consider seeking professional advice from a medical practitioner who can provide guidance on utilizing prescription medications to alleviate symptoms associated with nicotine withdrawal.

Do not concede

Similar to other forms of addiction, quitting smoking is a challenge that entails considerable difficulty.

Determination is required and it is imperative that you refrain from seeking justifications to indulge in smoking once more. Despite the possibility of setbacks, view this as an opportunity to enhance your commitment and exert greater effort.

CHAPTER FIVE

Studying the Causal Factors of Smoking

It is of utmost importance to acknowledge the situational factors that increase the susceptibility to relapse during the process of recovery. Do you operate in a workplace that enforces a smoking ban? Have you ever ingested alcoholic beverages, potentially leading to the emergence of a desire for a cigarette? Do you frequently find yourself in the presence of individuals who engage in smoking behaviors? Several factors attributing to a cigarette craving can be identified, and measures can be implemented to circumvent these factors. As an illustration, in cases where one is aware that being in the presence of individuals who engage in smoking would elicit an urge for smoking, it is imperative to minimize exposure to such environments.

Challenges and Encumbrances Faced in the Pursuit of Smoking Cessation

Ceasing the habit of smoking, as well as conquering the urge to smoke, can be achieved by implementing the following strategies:

I have continuously engaged in the act of resigning for a considerable duration of time. If you have previously undergone a successful cessation program of any nature, your likelihood of attaining success this time is significantly greater.

Engage in a comprehensive discussion with a professional tobacco-cessation counselor, such as a pharmacist or a dentist, who possesses the expertise to help you devise an effective strategy for quitting smoking. It is advisable to seek guidance from your dentist, pharmacy, physician, or healthcare practitioner for advice regarding the appropriate products to utilize.

Develop a strategic approach towards cessation. The article titled 'Cessation of

Smoking' offers a comprehensive selection of resources that may prove invaluable.

Select a date on which you intend to cease. Today marks the pivotal conclusion of your journey to overcome your smoking dependency. Please allocate a period of approximately one week for the cessation of this activity.

Commence by establishing a consensus with your family, acquaintances, and colleagues to abstain from the act of smoking. Kindly ask them to abstain from smoking in your vicinity. It might come as a pleasant surprise to discover that several individuals have acknowledged the significant enhancement in your health and are actively endorsing your choice to cease smoking.

Take proactive measures beforehand. Consider, for instance, the choice to relinquish ownership of your vehicle and transfer your residential phone service to the telecommunications company, alongside the decision to commence saving funds for dental care. In the event of a relapse, one would not be required to initiate the process anew.

Designate today as a day of ceasing the habit. Strive to refrain from dwelling on it. Kindly redirect your focus to another matter. Utilize the strategies elucidated in "A Comprehensive Quitting Framework" to assist you in devising your cessation plan.

Make Your Own Decisions. If you find the idea of relinquishing tobacco and nicotine unpleasant, it may be worth contemplating the substitution of chewing gum or nicotine gum as alternatives. These aforementioned products, along with others of similar nature, are readily available for purchase at your nearby pharmacy or drugstore establishment. If you require clarification or information regarding these or alternative nicotine replacement options, professional guidance can be sought from dental professionals, pharmacists or healthcare practitioners.

Health-related suggestions

Ceasing the habit of smoking can greatly contribute to enhancing one's physical wellbeing and minimize the likelihood of encountering subsequent health complications. Upon cessation of smoking, the subsequent actions can be pursued: "

It brings me great pleasure to acknowledge that your resolution to cease smoking and your firm dedication to relinquish this detrimental habit will undoubtedly lead to your genuine contentment.

It is imperative to consistently bear in mind to approach tasks progressively. If you apply the required diligence and display patience, you will have an opportunity to achieve success.

Consult with your physician.

Should you have any inquiries regarding cessation of smoking, it is advisable to seek guidance from a medical practitioner, dental specialist, or any other qualified healthcare expert. Numerous individuals exhibit a willingness to provide their assistance to you. Alternative approaches to enhance your well-being, besides smoking cessation, are discussed in the contents of 'Quit Smoking,' in case your healthcare provider does not advise quitting smoking or if you would rather explore alternative avenues for promoting your health.

Appropriate Approaches To Cease Smoking

By conducting online searches, one can discover various methods to cease tobacco consumption. There are individuals who assert that the utilization of pharmacological interventions facilitates nicotine cessation, while others contend that seeking guidance from a proficient counselor enables smoking cessation. Certain studies may assert that the initial approach holds superiority in smoking cessation, whereas alternative studies postulate the latter method as the optimal course of action. What precisely is the actuality?

In actuality, none of the aforementioned methods are incorrect. Certainly, the meticulous integration of these strategies will undeniably yield desired outcomes. In the present chapter, we shall delve into several prevalent methods of relinquishing the habit of smoking. It is highly advised that you refrain from adhering to a singular approach and instead employ a blend of two or more methods.

PHARMACOLOGICAL PRODUCTS

The primary concept underlying the utilization of pharmacological cessation agents is that they facilitate a gradual reduction of nicotine dependency. These products are designed to provide controlled amounts of nicotine, resulting in a reduced severity of nicotine withdrawal symptoms. Over an extended duration, one's physiology achieves complete reliance without the presence of nicotine. Consequently, you liberate yourself from the habit of smoking.

Cessation aids, known as nicotine replacement therapies, encompass options such as nicotine gum, nicotine patches, nicotine nasal sprays, and nicotine inhalers.

Directions to use:

Discontinue smoking altogether prior to commencing the use of the substitutes.

It is advisable to seek guidance from your therapist prior to determining the quit smoking products you intend to utilize.

Methodically taper the dosage of the substitutes.

Participate in a support program that offers group therapy sessions. Please elaborate on the efficacy of utilizing substitutions in your approach.

We strongly encourage you to cease both smoking and the use of any substitutes within a timeframe of 3-6 months.

ADVICE AND SUPPORT

Studies suggest that the provision of guidance and assistance by individuals in close proximity aids in achieving a sustained cessation of smoking. Per the guidance provided by the World Health Organization (WHO), it is recommended that therapists with appropriate professional training in the relevant field proactively undertake the task of supporting individuals in their efforts to quit smoking. It is essential for them to also furnish smokers with a comprehensive list of available resources that can offer the most effective assistance in their endeavor to cease smoking.

Numerous therapists employ the utilization of Cognitive Behavioral Therapy (CBT) to modify one's behavioral patterns and thought processes concerning smoking. This methodology entails the recognition and management of triggers, combined with recommendations for physical exercise and relaxation. In order to achieve efficacy, it is imperative that these techniques not only prioritize endeavors to achieve a temporary cessation of smoking, but also entail meticulous monitoring to prevent relapse among individuals.

A successful plan additionally offers various methodologies to aid in maintaining connectivity and staying on course. For instance, an effective strategy may encompass group dialogues, easy accessibility to online resources or articles pertaining to smoking cessation, and accounts of individuals who have triumphed in their efforts to quit smoking.

For example, the United Kingdom's NHS Smokefree initiative offers expert guidance, information, and assistance to individuals endeavoring to quit smoking. Such initiatives can additionally provide access to smoking cessation aids, such as nicotine patches, gum, as well as other quit smoking products like Champix or Zyban.

MEASURING AND RECORDING

The primary issue concerning individuals who smoke lies in their lack of precise awareness regarding the extent of their monetary expenditure on the purchase of tobacco products. Had they possessed the knowledge, the circumstances could have potentially taken a divergent course. Measuring and recording the number of cigarettes, and calculating the total amount of money you've spent on buying them till date will motivate you to quit your smoking.

Although the daily expense may not appear exorbitant, when projected over a month or even a year, the total amount that you uncover will surpass your initial expectations. The majority of smokers are likely to be astounded when confronted with such noteworthy statistics. This may prompt them to reconsider their smoking behavior. Research has indicated that a significant number of individuals who smoke express a desire to cease their smoking habit primarily in order to alleviate the financial burden associated with purchasing cigarettes. Therefore, this could potentially serve as a useful tool.

KNOWLEDGE AND INFORMATION

It is imperative for all smokers to possess a comprehensive understanding of accurate information regarding smoking and the associated drawbacks. A significant proportion of individuals who smoke are unaware of this information, consequently leading to their lack of motivation to cease smoking. If you maintain a genuine commitment to cease smoking, I would recommend conducting online research to explore the multitude of health complications encountered by individuals who engage in smoking. This will evoke fear regarding the potential adverse consequences you may encounter should you persist in your smoking habit.

The Hard Habit Awareness

The act of smoking, characterized by the combustion of a substance and the subsequent inhalation or consumption of its smoke, has long been embraced by a multitude of individuals across the globe. It is a prevalent and widely practiced form of drug consumption for recreational purposes. Tobacco is widely recognized as the most prevalent substance utilized, and its association with mortality is widely documented. Among the various manners in which tobacco is consumed, cigarette smoking stands out as the predominant method in all societal contexts. Annually, a significant number of individuals succumb to tobacco-related causes.

Diverse viewpoints exist with regards to smoking, which continues to evolve over time in different geographical locations. Certain individuals perceive it as sacred, refined, and even as a potential remedy, whereas others contend that it is sinful, indecent, and detrimental to one's well-being. In recent times, an abundance of medical research has substantiated the fact that smoking is a significant contributor to a myriad of health conditions such as heart attacks, lung cancer, and congenital malformations.

Individuals initiate smoking as a consequence of various factors. There exists a subset of individuals who perceive themselves as being more fashionable or stylish whilst partaking in the act of smoking. Others were simply swayed by the influence of their acquaintances and relatives who possess the propensity to engage in such behavior. Many individuals did not anticipate becoming addicted upon initially experimenting with smoking, which is why it is commonly asserted that abstaining from or avoiding it altogether would be relatively straightforward.

Ceasing the habit of smoking is undeniably a formidable endeavor, but it holds utmost significance for an individual's overall welfare. A considerable number of individuals possess an inadequate awareness or exhibit indifference toward the potential ramifications on their well-being. Smoking can induce various adverse effects such as anxiety, irritability, and weight gain, among others.

In contemporary times, there has been a widespread implementation of bans and regulations pertaining to smoking within numerous public venues. Advertising of tobacco products has been banned across all media platforms, including television, radio, and print publications. Indeed, it is widely acknowledged that the detrimental effects of smoking on one's health are common knowledge. Nevertheless, individuals persist in the habit of lighting their cigarettes and tobacco products freely, a behavior synonymous with addiction.

The Presence of Nicotine

The underlying cause of addiction lies in the consumption of nicotine. Despite strenuous efforts made by numerous individuals to cease consumption, their mental and physical faculties have become accustomed to the chemical compound inherent in tobacco. It bears resemblance to cocaine, heroin, and other varieties of addictive substances. Individuals experience a sense of normalcy upon using it and subsequently develop an overwhelming reliance, thereby impeding their ability to discontinue its usage.

Upon inhalation, smoke carries nicotine into the deep recesses of the lungs. It swiftly undergoes absorption into the bloodstream and subsequently gets conveyed throughout the entirety of the organism. The inhalation of nicotine from cigarette smoke expedites its passage into the brain, surpassing even the rapidity of drug absorption, thereby eliciting diverse effects on various bodily systems.

Additionally, it steers the smoker's attention away from the unpleasant emotions they are experiencing and elicits feelings of pleasure. This phenomenon elucidates the reasons behind individuals' continued engagement in smoking. It functions as a sedative. As individuals develop tolerance to nicotine, it is probable that they will engage in heightened tobacco consumption, consequently elevating the concentration of this chemical in their bloodstream. Upon completion of a cigarette, the nicotine concentration in their system initiates a gradual decline.

Their previously experienced positive emotions dissipate, leading to a renewed desire to engage in smoking behavior. Individuals may experience feelings of anxiety and irritability in the event of a delay in smoking.

When individuals attempt to discontinue a particular habit, they may encounter distinct physiological and psychological manifestations, commonly referred to as withdrawal symptoms, which necessitate effective management for successful cessation. If an individual engages in consistent smoking and abruptly ceases this activity, they will likely exhibit withdrawal symptoms, such as dizziness, irritability, anxiety, restlessness, headaches, and an augmented appetite. Typically, these symptoms persist for a duration of several days to multiple weeks. However, they will ultimately ameliorate as you consistently abstain from smoking each day.

There are multiple variables contributing to the duration of nicotine elimination from the body. Typically, the drug remains detectable in the system of habitual smokers for approximately 3 to 4 days following cessation.

It is imperative to understand that smoking has the potential to detrimentally affect the well-being of individuals in proximity to you, in addition to impacting your own health. Passive smoking, also known as secondhand smoke, emanates from the exhalation of smoke or the combustion of cigarettes. Additionally, it has the potential to induce migraines, provoke discomfort in the eyes, and contribute to the development of lung malignancies, which can ultimately result in fatality.

Quitting smoking can present a formidable challenge; however, with unwavering determination, individuals possess the capacity to overcome this entrenched habit. Mark Twain himself once expressed, "Abstaining from tobacco consumption is a task of ease." I have performed the task countless times."

Typically, individuals express concerns regarding the level of difficulty they might encounter when attempting to cease their engagement with a particular activity. It is important to bear in mind that achieving success may not occur expeditiously. It is imperative that you persist and persevere in your efforts. Many individuals have indeed achieved success, albeit after multiple attempts.

There exist several methods through which one can effectively cease smoking. It is imperative to comprehend the nature of the matter at hand and possess awareness of the available alternatives.

How to Quit Smoking

The prominent advertising display in Los Angeles effectively conveys the hazards of smoking to the public, although it may not have fully captivated their attention. It is possible that the message was influenced by a prominent personal connection, a reputable healthcare practitioner, or an unsettling anti-smoking advertisement.

According to expert analysis, a sudden unexpected occurrence or a strong emotional reaction has been identified as the primary catalyst for adopting smoking cessation techniques."

START =

Establish a predetermined date to cease the activity.

Inform your family, friends, and coworkers about your intention to resign.

A: Foresee and strategize for the obstacles you may encounter while endeavoring to cease.

Ensure the elimination of cigarettes and other tobacco products from your domicile, vehicle, and professional setting.

Please consult your healthcare provider for assistance in smoking cessation. Now let us delineate the procedures according to our own perspective.

Initially, it is essential for you to acknowledge the precipitating incident in your life that precipitated your resolution to resign. It is imperative to approach this matter with sensitivity, as it holds the potential to profoundly alter the course of your life, akin to experiencing a rebirth.

We recommend that you exclusively share your proposal with an individual who holds a significant and cherished place in your life.

Once more, we emphasize that there exists no substitute for an abrupt outburst. Therefore, it is possible that the act of discarding the cigarette finger grip may stem from an intimate and highly emotional setting, occurring either partially completed or subsequent to the final maneuver.

I kindly request that you refrain from expressing concern regarding the potential wastage of the remaining contents of the package. The money that

The loss incurred from that leftover cigarette is minimal when juxtaposed with the substantial savings you will experience in the upcoming days due to your transformative choice.

The most sophisticated approach to reaching a decision and subsequently communicating it to the general populace entails a certain degree of risk, which cannot be entirely ruled out, especially in instances where minor issues may arise and necessitate deferring the appointment.

Please be aware that there are numerous individuals who strongly discourage you from ceasing smoking.

These emotions may arise due to envy or apprehension regarding social detachment from the departure of a fellow individual who engages in smoking.

This announcement's sole positive aspect could potentially exert extra pressure on you to fulfill unnoticed obligations.

Consequently, we strongly advocate for the exercise of arbitrary decision-making. According to a report published by BBC News online, a study conducted by researchers at University College London involved a survey of over 1,900 individuals who were either current or former smokers. The findings revealed that approximately two-thirds of the participants who quit smoking abruptly achieved successful cessation for a period of at least six months, in comparison to less than half of those who meticulously planned their quitting strategy.

An equally critical concern pertains to the overall satisfaction that individuals derive from the acceptance of smoking by others in society.

They display a stronger inclination to rationalize the reasons behind their initiation of smoking rather than seeking the pivotal solution to the pressing query of why their smoking habit endures.

In this context, we aim to emphasize that smoking is an unhealthy behavior, often perpetuated out of habit rather than genuine enjoyment, in response to the prevalent inquiry, "What prompts individuals to engage in smoking?"

Nevertheless, it is plausible that you have disposed of the cigarette that was not fully extinguished or the partially filled pack in a manner infused with romance.

What happens after that? Your longstanding companion, known as nicotine, will not readily relinquish its hold on you due to its pervasive dissemination throughout the central nervous system, causing disruption to the entirety of your bodily functions.

Ceasing the habit of smoking can result in psychological complications leading to stress and potential relapse; however, seeking immediate assistance from a healthcare professional or counselor is crucial. Their guidance and support are indispensable in developing an effective plan for the future and administering appropriate medication, if deemed necessary.

If you are able to abstain from visiting the cigarette corner shop for more than one hour, it indicates successful completion of the task. Would you consider attending a lecture or a film screening concurrently with your immediate solution?

bears fruit? If you would like, you might consider patronizing a smoke-free dining establishment in the company of your loved ones to forego smoking on a few occasions. After dusk falls, you return to your residence without engaging in the purchase of a cigarette and endeavor to regain control over your anxious state of mind, opting to recline upon the bed instead. Kindly refrain from loitering on the balcony, as you were present there with a cigarette just yesterday.

If you are among those individuals who possess a propensity for accumulating a substantial quantity of cigarettes within the confines of their abode or workspace, in contemplation of unforeseen circumstances,

Please refrain from neglecting your duty to promptly dispose of all inventory in the waste bin.

Entering your bedroom. Please ensure that you are content with the plan to conduct an inventory the following day.

I will scarcely require any significant amount of time, nevertheless, permit me to endeavor until the subsequent morning.

It has been noted that individuals who engage in smoking tend to derive pleasure from witnessing the ascent of smoke surpassing the height of the flame.

They would refrain from smoking within a dimly lit room, as their preference lies in observing the elegant wisps of smoke rising. You desire to make a determination,

If the cigarette ignites, only the smoke rings are observable; however, should the flame ignite the depths of your psyche, then all may witness the emanation of these rings, for the accumulated energy is bound to project outward and inevitably be reflected in your surroundings.

May the dawn usher in revitalizing air for your being, enabling you to embrace the dawn's light as you embark upon a new chapter in your existence.

We guarantee that the sensation of dizziness will subside, allowing you to derive inspiration from the Sun, which ultimately invigorates both your physical and mental state. Take a deep breath.

Adverse Health Consequences Attributed to Tobacco Consumption

Adam and Eve disregarded God's warning and proceeded to partake in the precarious act of consuming the forbidden fruit.

Presently, the community has spared no efforts in addressing the negative implications of smoking, notwithstanding the public's awareness.

However, individuals persist in their smoking habits and a select few even discern a sense of romanticism behind the emblematic skull and Red Cross symbol, or the visual depictions of diseased lungs exhibited in medical clinics as a consequence of smoking.

Allow us to examine the composition of a cigarette enclosed within the white packaging.

Tobacco, being comprised primarily of Nicotine, exerts an impact on the human brain. It contains a total of forty-three carcinogenic substances and over four thousand chemical compounds, some of which possess sufficient toxicity to elicit desired effects within the human body. It comprises a total of four hundred distinct primary toxins, which are commonly found in widely employed wooden varnish and rat poison.

Therefore, it is imperative to take into account the impact.

Cigarettes serve as the primary catalyst for the most profound and feared epidemic of our era, primarily attributing to the onset of pulmonary malignancies. The research findings demonstrate that smoking is responsible for approximately 90% of lung cancer cases. The consumption of cigarettes affects the central nervous system, thus initiating the development of cancer in various organs including but not limited to the oral cavity, lips, pancreas, kidneys, stomach, urinary bladder, larynx, nasal passages, throat, and esophagus.

Smoking has been noted as a determinant factor for the development of leukemia.

Coughing and sneezing exacerbate significantly due to the habit of smoking.

Several studies have documented that smoking is associated with the development of Emphysema and chronic bronchitis.

What Is The Extent Of The Potential Harm It Can Cause?

Would you not consider instead... keeping vigilant, ensuring that all your lights are on, securing the entrances and windows, and perhaps wielding a dependable baseball bat or golf club? You and your household can be assured that no harm will come to you, or, at the very least, not without encountering resistance.

The image may fall on either end of the spectrum, ranging from a highly simplified representation to an exceptionally captivating depiction, yet it is highly probable that you comprehend its essence. Protecting oneself and one's family from harm is a task that typically comes instinctively to most individuals. We instill in our children the importance of practicing caution when crossing the road and avoiding conversations with unfamiliar individuals, as well as promoting the utilization of seat belts and the precautionary measure of securing windows and doors during nighttime.

Why is it, then, that this inclination towards safety seems to be disregarded when it pertains to the practice of smoking cigarettes? This practice causes harm not only to the individual partaking in it, but also to all those in proximity who are exposed to secondhand smoke.

To what extent does the situation exhibit a considerable level of severity? What is the extent of impact that an individual carries?

Retain awareness of crucial facts and pertinent statistical data pertaining to smoking.

The act of cigarette smoking imposes a significant economic burden on the United States, amounting to a staggering $167 billion annually. This cost encompasses various aspects, including $92 billion in productivity losses caused by premature deaths and $75 billion in direct healthcare expenses. On average, each adult smoker is responsible for an estimated financial impact of $3,702.

May I inquire if you possess the sum of $3,702 readily available within your possession? Alternatively, would you consider terminating your checking account today, with both convenience and ease? However, this amount represents the annual cost incurred by each individual who smokes cigarettes.

The make-up of cigarettes.

It is imperative to bear this in mind due to the fact that inevitably there will always be illnesses and health issues, many of which are solely attributable to genetics or other circumstances beyond control. As previously indicated, in the event that one becomes aware of an individual intending harm towards oneself or one's family, every measure would be taken to thwart their intentions. Regarding cigarette smoking, however, people often permit the practice into their residences without considering its detrimental nature and the harm it inflicts upon them and their families.

The # 1 deadly.

In contemporary times, cigarettes are comprised of constituents beyond mere tobacco. Additional chemicals are commonly incorporated during the production process, enhancing the addictive properties of the cigarette. Indeed, there exists a total of 599 ingredients present in cigarettes. However, as the material undergoes combustion and subsequent changes in chemical composition, the act of smoking generates over 4,000 chemical compounds.

Cigarette smoking has been officially identified as the top preventable cause of death worldwide. What this implies is that among the global incidents of preventable death, cigarette smoking is one of the most prevalent. Among the various modifications that one can undertake to enhance and safeguard their well-being, such as weight loss, adopting a healthy diet, engaging in regular physical activity, receiving necessary vaccinations, and more, smoking occupies the foremost position.

Cigarette smoking is responsible for approximately 90% of fatalities caused by lung cancer, as well as over 80% of cases of Chronic Obstructive Pulmonary Disease (COPD), which includes emphysema and bronchitis. Similarly, these profoundly consequential respiratory ailments often necessitate transplantation or result in mortality.

With regards to 8.6 million individuals in the United States, it is worth noting that they have been afflicted by at least one significant ailment attributed to the act of smoking. This suggests that for each individual who succumbs to an illness caused by smoking, there are an additional 20 individuals who endure at least one severe ailment linked to tobacco use.

Smoking-related ailments claim the lives of approximately 438,000 individuals in the United States annually, including those who are indirectly affected, such as premature infants born as a result of prenatal maternal smoking and individuals exposed to the harmful effects of secondhand smoke. This indicates that approximately 500,000 Americans annually succumb to tobacco-related diseases and causes, in their own right.

Presently, please consider a group of twenty individuals whom you are acquainted with. Presently, one must consider the unfortunate plight of these individuals who are suffering greatly due to the effects of your tobacco consumption.

Cigarette smoking in numbers.

Cigarette smoke contains carbon monoxide gas, nitrogen oxides, hydrogen cyanide, formaldehyde, and ammonia. There exist a total of forty-three widely recognized health risks present in mainstream smoke, sidestream smoke, or both.

Please be advised that the components within cigarettes are utilized in the production of various other common household items. Consider whether you would choose to consume any of these substances.

Mothballs are composed of naphthalenes, which are also found in cigarettes. This examined toxic substance induces both reproductive dysfunction and cognitive impairment.

It is worth considering whether you have any preference for inhaling the identical chemical constituents present in nail polish remover, melted plastic, rodenticides, batteries, and mothballs. However, the coexisting elements in each cigarette, alongside tar, ammonia, nicotine, and assorted pollutants.

There exists a significant disparity of approximately 85% in the prevalence of erectile dysfunction between male smokers and non-smokers, with cigarette smoking being a prominent contributing factor to the development of impotence. Cigarette smoking induces erectile dysfunction by promoting arterial constriction.

The arsenic utilized for rat extermination is also present in cigarettes. It induces pronounced pulmonary distress, aberrations in cardiac rhythm, and a host of diverse additional manifestations.

The cadmium in batteries is exceptionally harmful when located in cigarettes as well as lead to kidney harm.

Both adhesive and cigarettes contain toluene, a hazardous substance that induces euphoria and causes irritation of the respiratory tract and lungs.

Given that these toxins circulate within the bloodstream, they significantly impact the cardiovascular system, thus smoking cigarettes is widely regarded as a prominent contributor to cardiovascular ailments.

What cigarettes really damage.

Vice versa. The toxins found in cigarettes are efficiently disseminated throughout the body and are readily absorbed into the bloodstream, permeating nearly every pore and cell.

Numerous individuals acknowledge the extensive harm cigarettes cause to the respiratory system and readily associate their usage with the development of lung cancer. Is this the sole substantial condition that is activated by the consumption of cigarette smoking?

The toxic phenol compound found in both plastics and cigarettes has the potential to induce kidney and liver damage, in addition to causing a decrease in blood pressure levels, thereby resulting in severe illness and potentially mortality.

Tar is a constituent present in road surfaces, as well as in tires and cigarettes. A habitual smoker who consumes two packs of cigarettes per day inhales approximately one gram of tar on a daily basis. That constitutes a liter of viscous substance inhaled annually.

Acetone is a constituent found in nail polish remover as well as tobacco products. It is a harsh chemical that exacerbates respiratory function and has the potential to induce carcinogenesis.

The presence of ammonia in bleach accelerates the degradation of pure nicotine in cigarette shipments, thereby altering the measured levels of tar in cigarettes and causing them to appear lower.

Several other conditions associated with the consumption of tobacco cigarettes include:

Engaging in physical exercise helps achieve this objective, as it enables you to spend time outdoors and away from tempting indulgences. Additionally, exercise plays a vital role in restoring your metabolism to its optimal functioning state. The increased physical activity will undoubtedly contribute to weight management, subsequently reducing the likelihood of cigarette relapse.

Once again, you are faced with the need to make challenging decisions. What holds greater significance for you, the well-being and health of yourself, your family, or the supposed friendship in question? It is important to acknowledge that a true companion is an individual who supports your endeavors that are advantageous to you. Therefore, a genuine friend, regardless of their duration of smoking, will exhibit respect for your decision and your surroundings.

Furthermore, numerous individuals have attested to experiencing positive results by consuming mint leaves in a manner akin to chewing gum. This is an organic remedy that not only keeps your mouth active, but also ensures your breath remains pleasantly fresh.

Furthermore, it is highly enticing to seize opportunities in order to replace those weary companions. This could pose a significant setback for anyone attempting to quit, particularly when the food choices they gravitate towards are high in fat and calories. Indulging in salted chips, crackers, snacks, and sugary treats like cookies and cupcakes will not be any more advantageous to your health than smoking cigarettes.

You may currently need to consider the specific social activities you engage in and the environments you frequent, as these may be contributing to your inclination to smoke. Consider exploring alternatives to bars, as we have previously deliberated, or seeking alternative recreational activities.

Affair.

Please ascertain if your team would be willing to take rest in the designated non-smoking section of a dining establishment, or alternatively, if they would be open to altering their plans in order to locate a club or bar that offers a non-smoking area.

By conscientiously monitoring your dietary intake and food choices, you will not only prevent any undesirable weight gain, but also experience an overall improvement in well-being. This positive transformation will serve as an additional motivator in adhering to your newfound healthy habit of abstaining from smoking. Retrieve a pen and paper and commence with the preparation of the checklist immediately. Customize it according to your personal preferences and choices, but ensure that your choice of snacks and meal items are nutritious and organic.

Certainly, it is not feasible to keep your hands occupied in the vehicle, however you might consider listening to an audiobook instead. Ensuring the engagement of your mind is the initial step in ensuring the occupation of your hands.

One further benefit of exercising is that it enhances pulmonary function and promotes efficient blood circulation. One of the functions of our blood is to nourish the cells of the body, as well as eliminate waste materials including dead cells and various toxins.

Add a generous amount of fiery hot sauce to enhance the flavor of a vegan chili recipe or to accompany your tacos. Indulge in the experience of trying sushi, accompanied by a small touch of wasabi or ginger.

It would be advantageous at this moment to procure a sheet of paper and subsequently delineate those times as a comprehensive inventory. Please provide examples of social gatherings in which you find yourself engaging, such as the customary game of poker with your male acquaintances, or the Friday evenings when the female group gathers for martinis. Leave absolutely nothing out.

Now that you have compiled a list, consider the actions you can take to extricate yourself from the immediate habit of reaching for a cigarette. If this is the designated time you allocate for conversing with your partner or household, it is advisable to move to a separate room.

Examine your dietary regimen and nutritional intake.

Undoubtedly, given that this habitual manner of communication upon departure from a location had become deeply ingrained within her psyche, she exhibited a complete lack of conscious awareness regarding her actions. It appears as though her arm was autonomously in control, instinctively reaching for the button regardless of her intentions.

When endeavoring to cease the habit of smoking cigarettes, it is advisable to consistently consume ample amounts of water and ensure continual hydration. Cigarette smoking has effectively constricted your blood vessels and inflicted considerable damage to your circulatory system; the only viable remedy for this dire situation is ample hydration.

Moreover, there exists evidence suggesting a correlation between the act of smoking tobacco and the development of leukemia, early onset of Alzheimer's disease, as well as birth defects in infants born to women who smoke during pregnancy.

One might also consider venturing beyond their comfort zone and sampling unfamiliar flavors that they have yet to experience. Alternatively, if you have a preference for Chinese cuisine, kindly request that they enhance the spiciness level of the dish to your liking.

There is likely a considerable amount that can be asserted regarding the value and benefits of exercise when one is endeavoring to quit smoking.

Smoking is also considered one of the most costly indulgences that an individual can engage in, and there exist several digital tools designed to demonstrate precisely the extent of one's daily, weekly, and annual expenditures on tobacco consumption.

Please refer to the subsequent figures, assuming a unit price of $3.50 per pack of cigarettes (in US dollars):.

You may also have an inclination to discover nutritious recipes and accompanying dishes that will help you maintain optimal physical condition. Please consider replacing your white bread with whole grain or whole wheat bread.

Explore the options of delightfully flavored gums, such as those infused with warm cinnamon or refreshing peppermint. The additional flavor will undoubtedly aid in reducing the remaining taste of tobacco, and once again, it will impart a fresh and enticing flavor to your palate.

When it comes to smoking cigarettes, it is necessary to acknowledge the immense difficulty in breaking a deeply ingrained physical habit. Consider the habitual instances during the course of the day when one instinctively reaches for a cigarette, devoid of conscious thought, such as following a meal, while commuting to work in the morning, or even subsequent to engaging in sexual activity. Opportunities are it's not that you truly desire that cigarette, you're merely responding to your routine.

Expect to encounter resistance, in fact, it is highly probable that you will encounter substantial resistance from individuals who have been habituated to the ability to relax with a cigarette or cigar at any place or time. Certain acquaintances may also begin to discourage your participation or opt to avoid such events.

The daily consumption of cigarettes	The weekly amount of money invested	The monthly amount of money invested	The yearly amount of money invested
6 (1/2 pack)	$7.35	$31.50	$383.25
12 (pack)	$14.70	$62.10	$766.50
24 (2 packs)	$29.40	$125.10	$1,532.10

Kindly communicate transparently about your conscientious efforts to quit smoking and the profound challenges associated with being in the company of individuals engaged in smoking activities. You are not requesting the cessation of their smoking habit as well – however, it would be highly beneficial for their well-being if they so desired, and you can certainly support each other in this endeavor. In the event that they need to smoke, kindly ask them to inform you, and you may both take a brief recess to accommodate their needs.

Moreover, another challenge that numerous individuals encounter while striving to quit smoking cigarettes is the situations in which they have recently become accustomed to smoking, such as social gatherings at bars or nightclubs. The act of tobacco consumption and smoking tend to be closely associated, particularly in social settings where one is surrounded by individuals engaging in the same behavior.

Identify it's a routine.

Except in the case of being the designated host or organizer of these events. It may be opportune to inform your guests that your residence currently adheres to a smoke-free policy, requiring them to relocate outdoors, specifically onto the patio or veranda, should they wish to smoke.

Additionally, contemplate the significant financial resources that could be more efficiently allocated to your mortgage or car installment, directed towards credit card payments or your children's education fund, or indulged in activities that bring greater pleasure than smoking.

As previously stated, if you have developed a habitual tendency of lounging after a meal accompanied by a cigarette, it is now appropriate to initiate a routine of engaging in brisk walks around the neighborhood. If you are accustomed to experiencing a final discomfort before retiring for the night, endeavor to engage in a domestic endeavor instead, such as attending to dishwashing, tending to laundry, performing a concise cleaning of the bathroom, or any other activity that is not overly strenuous yet can keep you occupied.

Various other all-natural remedies.

Working out.

Many individuals who have been smokers for an extended period frequently express dissatisfaction with the diminished taste of various foods. This can be attributed to the detrimental effects that cigarette smoke has inflicted upon the taste buds and oral cavity. The inhalation of this smoke can have an adverse effect on one's palate, resulting in a lessened perception of flavor in certain types of food.

Establish a novel routine of carrying these items with you throughout the duration of the day. If a refrigerator is available at the workplace, ensure to supply it with both oranges and apples, while also keeping a supply of trail mix stored in a desk drawer.

Renal malignancies

Malignant cells within the larynx

Malignant cells located in the craniofacial region.

Bust cancer cells

Liver cancer cells

Cervical cancer cells

Strokes

Outer vascular illness

Respiratory disease

Cataracts

Cognitive disorder

In terms of veracity, it is worth noting that cigarettes contain more than 599 ingredients. However, the process of combustion alters the chemical composition of substances, giving rise to more than 4,000 chemical compounds when smoking cigarettes.

Could you kindly clarify the specific choice that is being referred to? It is of utmost importance at this juncture to derive pleasure from the foods and beverages one consumes while striving to quit. You can effectively leverage these cravings by opting for nutritious and well-balanced alternatives.

One of the most formidable aspects of attempting to cease smoking is encountered when socializing with friends who are smoking, or being in smoke-filled environments such as bars, restaurants, or pubs. Exactly what to do?

Enhanced blood circulation suggests that toxins are being efficiently expelled from your system at a higher frequency. The residual toxins and addictive components present in cigarettes continue to persist in your body for an extended period following your last inhalation. Therefore, engaging in physical exercise and enhancing your blood circulation can expedite their elimination from your system.

It is further recommended that you consider taking Epsom salt baths as they are believed to facilitate the removal of tar and nicotine from your body.

An assortment of various fruits, particularly apples, pears, kiwi, watermelon, along with citrus fruits. These food varieties possess a notable water content, thereby aiding in the sustenance of your satiety levels.

Vegetables that can be consumed in their natural state, including carrots or celery. Please consider incorporating low-fat or low-calorie alternatives like Cattle ranch salad dressing or hummus as dips, and also provide bite-sized vegetables such as broccoli, cauliflower, or other similar options.

www.ingramcontent.com/pod-product-compliance
Lightning Source LLC
Chambersburg PA
CBHW050410120526
44590CB00015B/1900